# Introduction

## Join Kathy Orta Files on the creative adventure of mini al...

Have you ever wanted to scrapbook, but actually wanted to feel like you completed a project? That's what a mini album is all about—a paper-crafting project with a beginning and an end. Record your memories and tell your stories in a compact-size scrapbook that will keep the viewer wanting more with every turn of the page. These fun and interactive mini albums will house all of the wonderful moments captured and all of the memorabilia collected along your journey. And the best part is that you can display this wonderful keepsake in your home or make it a treasured gift. Remember and relive those unforgettable moments for years to come.

# Meet the Designer

**Kathy Orta Files** is an experienced teacher, educator and creative inspirer. Eight years ago, she began sharing her knowledge of preserving memories through workshops and her blog. Her love for paper crafting and home decor started her on a journey of creating unique scrapbooks and paper crafts that can be enjoyed in homes as decorative accents. With years of experience in the paper-crafting field, Kathy has created many 3-D projects, home decor pieces, custom mini albums and more than 100 educational classes. You can see Kathy's work on her website, www.paperphenomenon.com, and featured online in numerous scrapbooking blogs.

Kathy has had the pleasure of designing for Cricut at Provo Craft's shows and TV events, for Tim Holtz' booths at CHA and for Annie's Online Classes.

She resides in sunny Florida with her family and enjoys sharing her passion for the creative arts with fellow crafters and friends.

# Contents

# General Instructions

Paper crafting is fun and creative. In these general instructions, Kathy has shared some hints, tips and techniques that will help you complete your mini scrapbook projects successfully.

## Cutting

Use a 12-inch paper trimmer with a sharp blade to create clean cuts. When cutting chipboard, take several light passes until the blade penetrates the chipboard completely. When cutting paper or cardstock, hold the piece firmly to the cutting surface and slide the blade from top to bottom in a smooth action.

Take time to plan cuts to get the most pieces from each piece of chipboard, paper or cardstock. Accurate measuring and cutting will make these projects much easier to assemble.

## Labeling Cut Pieces

Label each cut piece with the corresponding alphabet or name. Keep the label with the piece throughout the assembly process. Labeling will allow you to follow the instructions quickly and efficiently.

## Scoring

There are multiple scoring boards available at retail or online. When scoring, make sure to follow the manufacturer's instructions for using the board. A 12 x 12-inch scoring board and tool with scoring lines every ⅛ inch is recommended to create the projects in this book.

The instructions for each album project will explain which edge of the paper, cardstock or chipboard to press against the top of the scoring board. Correct placement is important to ensure the scored lines are being made on the correct edge of the cut piece.

For best scoring results, hold the scoring tool at a 45-degree angle to the surface, not on the tip like a pencil would be held. *Note: Holding the scoring tool so the tip of the tool is doing the scoring can cut thin patterned papers and cardstock.* Use even pressure and draw the tool down the paper. When scoring thinner papers and cardstock, make sure to apply light pressure as pressing too hard can cut paper instead of scoring it. For heavy-weight cardstock, score twice over the score line. If scoring patterned paper or cardstock with a white core, lower the angle of the scoring tool to avoid cracking or cutting through your paper.

## Folding

When scoring paper, cardstock or chipboard, the fibers are being spread to help create a crisp finished fold.

Folds that face downward are commonly called valley folds. Folds that face upward are called mountain folds. In some cases, it is recommended to fold the scored piece so the debossed score line is on the outside of the fold and the embossed ridge is on the inside of the fold. ***Note:*** *For the projects in this publication it is not important to fold on a score line one way or another.*

However, for a fold like an accordion fold, every other score should be completed on the back side of the paper.

## Burnishing

Use a bone folder or the scoring tool to burnish all folds. This will create a crisp crease in the fold and will help eliminate bulk and aid in creating a crisper fold.

## Adhesives

We recommend using Scor-Tape™ for the projects in this book. Scor-Tape™ is a premium, double-sided adhesive that is acid-free, heat-resistant and incredibly sticky. Its tight bond makes it the perfect permanent adhesive for making albums. Scor-Tape™ is paper backed, which means it can be torn by hand with no need for scissors or sharp blades. This double-sided adhesive comes in multiple widths. We used the ¼-inch-wide Scor-Tape™ for these projects.

## Folded & Extended Positions

In many of these projects, the instructions will state to apply double-sided adhesive to the flaps in the folded position. In the folded position, fold and burnish along the score lines. Keep the folds facing you and apply the double-sided adhesive (Folded Position).

If instructed to place double-sided adhesive in the extended position, score, fold and burnish as instructed, then flatten the piece to its original shape and size. Apply the double-sided adhesive to the outside area created by the score (Extended Position).

> **Tip**
> *It is important to avoid placing double-sided adhesive on the scored line unless instructed to do so.*

## Tapering to Reduce Bulk

When creating hinges, pockets and flaps, reduce the bulk at corners by cutting out or tapering corners. Tapering each end of the hinges will help them slide easily into the pockets. Only remove a taper about ¼ inch wide (Taper Hinge End).

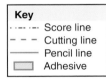

**Key**
- ·—·—· Score line
- – – – Cutting line
- —— Pencil line
- ▭ Adhesive

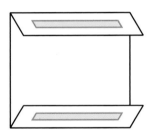

**Folded Position**

**Extended Position**

**Taper Hinge End**

When two score lines cross, it creates a square in the corner. Use a pair of scissors to cut along the score line to the point where they intersect. Remove the square. This will reduce the bulk when the folds are made to create the pocket (Remove Square).

Tapering the edges of flaps will reduce bulk. A ½-inch taper is usually sufficient to reduce bulk. The taper also helps disguise any irregularities in cutting (Taper Flap).

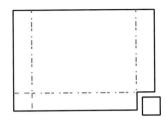

**Remove Square**

**Taper Flap**

### Decorating & Embellishing

Everyone likes to choose decorative and patterned papers that fit their taste and the theme of their album. Therefore, this book gives instructions for making the basic album and allows you to decorate and embellish as you desire. Each project gives sources for papers used.

There are some steps in the album building process where it is necessary to place a patterned paper before continuing the assembly process. In those cases, the instructions advise you to cut and adhere the patterned paper before proceeding with the next step. When the album is completed, decorate with patterned papers and embellishments as desired, matching the album to your specific tastes or to those of the person to whom you will give the album. Cut the layering papers a ¼-inch smaller width and height than the base it will be adhered to and the result will be a ⅛-inch border. This border will add depth to the layering.

Use a corner rounder or scissors to round some of the corners on flaps of the album. This will add interest and help keep square edges from becoming damaged when viewing the album.

### Mitered Corners

Several of the projects in this book use chipboard to create the sturdy base of the album. The chipboard is covered with patterned paper. A miter is created at the corner of the paper to reduce bulk for folding.

To miter the corner, follow the measurement instructions on each project. Mark the paper and draw a diagonal line. The diagonal line should be about ⅛ inch away from the corner of the chipboard. This space allows you to completely cover the corner when folding paper.

Tightly fold and adhere the paper over the chipboard on the top edge first. Use a bone folder or your fingernail to burnish down the small fold that extends past the chipboard corner. Fold the next side in the same manner, working your way around the entire four sides. ❮

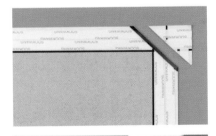

# Mini Treasures

This mini album is perfect to slide into your purse to show off all those special photos of kids or grandkids.

## Materials
› 3 (12 x 12-inch) solid cardstock
› Patterned paper to decorate as desired
› Desired stickers
› Desired embellishments
› Paper trimmer
› Scoring board
› Bone folder
› Scissors
› Ruler
› Punches: ¼-inch hole, corner rounder (optional)
› Double-sided adhesive

*Project note: Refer to General Instructions for specific techniques as needed. Contrasting cardstock has been used in photos to aid in visual instructions. Label all cut pieces with the corresponding letter to help identify pieces for scoring and assembly.*

## Pieces to Cut
### Solid Cardstock

One 11 x 8½ inches (A)

Two 4 x 8¼ inches (B)

Two 5 x 3 inches (C)

One 5 x 3½ inches (D)

One 4 x 6 inches (E)

One 3 x 4½ inches (F)

## Patterned Paper

Two 4¾ x 7¼ inches (G)

Two 3¾ x 7 inches (H)

Three 3¾ x 2¾ inches (I)

One 3¼ x 5¼ inches (J)

One 2¼ x 3¾ inches (K)

## Scoring Instructions

**1.** Place long edge of A against top of scoring board. Score at ½-inch, 5½-inch and 10½-inch marks. Place short edge against top of scoring board. Score at ½-inch and 8-inch marks.

**2.** Place long edge of B against top of scoring board. Score at ½-inch and 8-inch marks. Repeat for second piece.

**3.** Place long edge of C against top of scoring board. Score at ½-inch and 4½-inch marks. Repeat for second piece.

**4.** Place long edge of D against top of scoring board. Score at ½-inch and 4½-inch marks. Place short edge against top of scoring board. Score at ½-inch mark.

**5.** Place long edge of E against top of scoring board. Score at ½-inch mark. Place short edge against top of scoring board. Score at ½-inch mark.

**6.** Place long edge of F against top of scoring board. Score at ½-inch mark. Place short edge against top of scoring board. Score at ½-inch mark.

## Assembly Instructions

**1.** On piece A, cut out the four squares created by the overlapping score marks. Fold along score lines. Flatten to original size. Center and adhere one piece G to each side. Do not cover center score. Set aside (Photo 1).

**2.** Fold B along score lines. Place double-sided adhesive on flaps in the Folded Position (page 4). Repeat for second piece B.

**3.** Adhere one piece B to left-hand side of A as shown. Repeat for second pocket B on right-hand side of A. Center and adhere one piece H to each piece B (Photo 2).

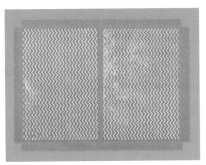

[ Photo 1 ]

[ Photo 2 ]

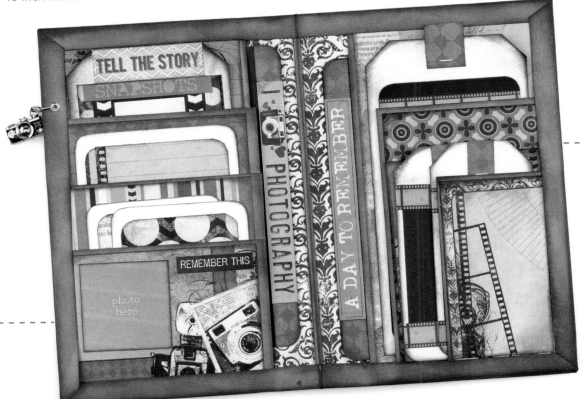

[ Photo 3 ]

[ Photo 4 ]

[ Photo 5 ]

[ Photo 6 ]

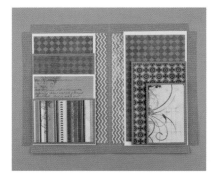

[ Photo 7 ]

**4.** Fold C along score lines. Place double-sided adhesive on flaps in the Folded Position. Repeat for second piece C. **Note:** *If pockets with closed bottoms are desired, place a line of adhesive along one long edge between the score lines. This edge will become the bottom of the pocket.*

**5.** Measure down 1¼ inches from top on both sides of left-hand pocket B and make a pencil mark. Lightly draw a line between the two marks. Adhere one piece C, lining up top with pencil mark so opening faces top of album. Center and adhere one piece I to C (Photo 3).

**6.** Overlap second pocket C 1¼ inches down from top of first pocket C. Center and adhere one piece I to second piece C (Photo 4).

**7.** On D, cut out squares created by overlapping score lines. Fold along score lines. Place double-sided adhesive on flaps in the folded position. Adhere D to bottom of left-hand pocket B just slightly

above the bottom fold line. **Note:** *Adhering slightly above the fold of B will reduce the bulk.* Center and adhere third piece I to D (Photo 5).

**8.** On E, cut out the square created by the overlapping score lines. Fold two edges of E at score lines to create a pocket that opens to the left. Place double-sided adhesive on flaps in the Folded Position. Adhere to right-hand side B pocket slightly above fold with opening facing to the left. Center and adhere J to E (Photo 6).

**9.** On F, cut out the square created by the overlapping score lines. Fold along score lines to create a pocket that opens to the left. Place double-sided adhesive on flaps in the Folded Position. Adhere to right-hand side of E with opening facing to the left. Center and adhere K to F (Photo 7).

*Make sure your measurements are precise, an extra ⅛ inch can make the difference between a scrapbook that fits together correctly and one that bulges or is off-centered.*

 Tip

**10.** Apply double-sided adhesive to the flaps of A, placing adhesive so it runs along the outer edges of the flap. Fold flaps in on score line to cover all edges. Burnish well. Fold album along center score line to close.

**11.** Decorate outside of album with patterned paper, embellishments and stickers as desired. ❮

***Sources:*** *Mama-razzi2 patterned paper, stickers and embellishments from Bo-Bunny Press; scoring board and bone folder from Martha Stewart Crafts; paper trimmer from Fiskars; craft knife from Prima Marketing; Scor-Tape™ double-sided adhesive from Scor-Pal Products.*

# Bonus Add-Ons

- *You can further embellish your album with tags that slide into the pockets. Make as many tags as desired to hold photos, journaling and memorabilia.*
- ***Large Tag:*** *Cut 4¼ x 6-inch piece cardstock. Round all four corners. Embellish as desired. Slide into large pocket in album.*
- ***Medium Tag:*** *Cut 3 x 6¼-inch piece cardstock. Taper top two corners to create tag shape. Punch ¼-inch hole in center. Embellish as desired.*
- ***Small Tag:*** *Cut 2½ x 3¾-inch piece cardstock. Round all four corners. Embellish as desired.*

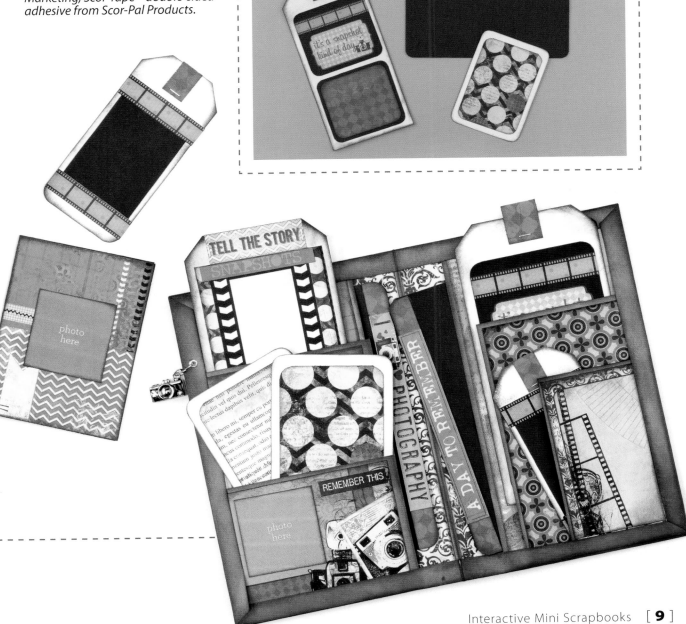

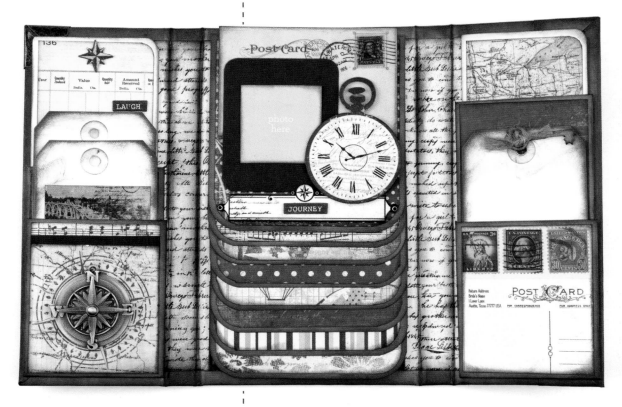

# Flipped Out

Small enough to fit in your favorite bag, this mini album features flip-up pages to hold maximum photos in a minimum space.

## Materials

> › 1 (12 x 12-inch) chipboard
> › 4 (12 x 12-inch) brown cardstock
> › 1 (12 x 12-inch) patterned paper, plus pieces to decorate as desired
> › Sticky notes
> › ¾-inch hinge clip embellishment
> › Swivel clasp with chain and jump rings
> › Desired themed embellishments: metal, chipboard
> › ¼-inch eyelet
> › Punches: ¼-inch hole (or awl), corner rounder
> › Eyelet-setting tool (optional)
> › Ruler
> › Paper trimmer
> › Scissors
> › Scoring board
> › Bone folder
> › Craft knife
> › Quick-drying liquid adhesive
> › ¼-inch-wide double-sided adhesive

***Project note:*** *Refer to General Instructions for specific techniques as needed. Contrasting cardstock has been used in photos to aid in visual instructions. Use sticky notes to label all cut pieces with the corresponding letter to help identify pieces for scoring and assembly.*

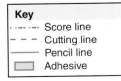

**Key**

-·-·- Score line
- - - Cutting line
——— Pencil line
▭ Adhesive

## Pieces to Cut

### Chipboard

Two 3 x 8 inches (A)

Two 8 x ½ inches (B)

One 4½ x 8 inches (C)

### Cardstock

One 12 x 9½ inches (D)

One 2½ x 9½ inches (E)

Seven 4¼ x 5 inches (F)

Four 4 x 4½ inches (G)

### Patterned Paper

One 12 x 7½ inches (H)

## Scoring Instructions

**1.** Place long edge of F against top of scoring board. Score at ½-inch mark. Repeat for remaining pieces.

**2.** Place long edge of G against top of scoring board. Score at ½-inch and 4-inch marks. Repeat for remaining pieces. Place short edge against top of scoring board. Score at ½-inch and 3½-inch marks. Repeat for remaining pieces.

## Assembly Instructions

**1.** Apply double-sided adhesive along one long edge of E.

**2.** Adhere E to a short edge of D, overlapping by ½ inch to make a 14 x 9½-inch piece. Label as Cover.

**3.** On Cover, measure and mark ¾ inch from bottom, top and both sides. Draw a line connecting marks (Fig. 1).

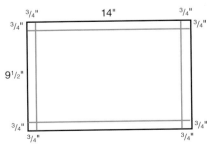

**Fig. 1**

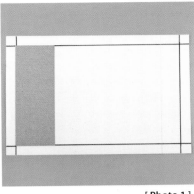

[ Photo 1 ]

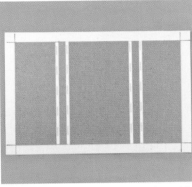

[ Photo 2 ]

**4.** Apply double-sided adhesive to one side of chipboard pieces A, B and C. Adhere one piece A to left edge of Cover piece aligning at pencil marks (Photo 1).

**5.** Adhere the following in order from left to right to Cover piece, keeping top and bottom aligned with pencil marks: ¼-inch-wide tape, one piece B, ¼-inch-wide tape, C, ¼-wide-tape, second piece B, ¼-inch-wide tape and second piece A (Photo 2). ***Note:*** *If your last piece of chipboard hangs over your line a little, that is OK. There is enough margin of cardstock to fold over.*

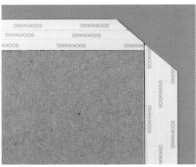

[ Photo 3 ]

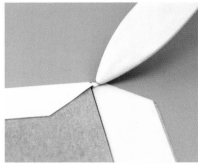

[ Photo 4 ]

[ Photo 5 ]

**6.** Apply tape to the perimeter of Cover piece. Measure 1¼ inches from each corner on edge of cardstock and make a pencil mark. Draw a diagonal line between marks connecting them. There should be about ⅛ inch between the line and the corner of your chipboard. Adjust line if necessary before cutting miter. Repeat for all four corners and cut along lines (Photo 3).

**7.** Remove the tape backing from around the perimeter of the Cover piece and from in between the chipboard pieces. Fold one long edge of cardstock tightly over the chipboard and press down to secure. Note the excess cardstock at the miter. Press this down with a bone folder or your fingernail to secure around the corner of the chipboard. Fold the next side. Work your way around the Cover, preparing each corner in the same manner (Photo 4).

**8.** Cover the back side of H liberally with double-sided adhesive, making sure to apply adhesive around the entire perimeter of the cardstock. Center and adhere H to chipboard side of Cover. Press tightly to chipboard and push down into adhesive along ½-inch

pieces of chipboard. This is where your album will fold and you want the paper to be well adhered in that area. *Note: After adhering two pieces together, burnish the area with your bone folder to strengthen the bond of the adhesive.* Carefully fold both ends of album toward center to identify center area (Photo 5).

**9.** Fold F along score line. Repeat for remaining F pieces.

**10.** Round two corners on the end opposite the score if desired. Place tape along the scored edge with flap in the Folded Position (page 4). Repeat for remaining pieces F (Fig. 2).

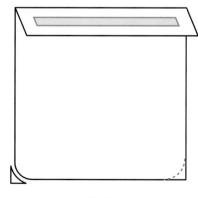

**Fig. 2**

**Key**

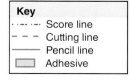

-·--·-- Score line
- - - - Cutting line
——— Pencil line
▭ Adhesive

[ Photo 6 ]

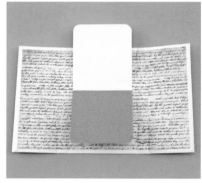

[ Photo 7 ]

**11.** Adhere F to inside center section of album so that edge opposite the score is about ⅛ inch above bottom edge of album (Photo 6).

**12.** Adhere remaining six F pieces to album, lining up each tab with the top of the previous piece. Decorate flaps with patterned paper as desired (Photo 7).

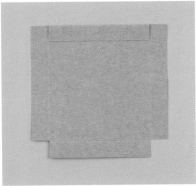

[ Photo 8 ]

**13.** On one piece G, cut out the four squares created by the overlapping score marks. In the Extended Position (page 4), apply tape across the top flap along 4-inch edge. Fold and adhere. This creates a folded top for your pocket. Repeat for remaining three G pieces (Photo 8).

**14.** Fold remaining three sides of G piece along scored lines. Place tape on flaps in the Folded Position (page 4). ***Note:*** *Make sure that the flaps are folded to the same side as the folded top.* Repeat for remaining three pieces G (Fig. 3).

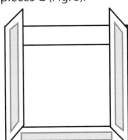

**Fig. 3**

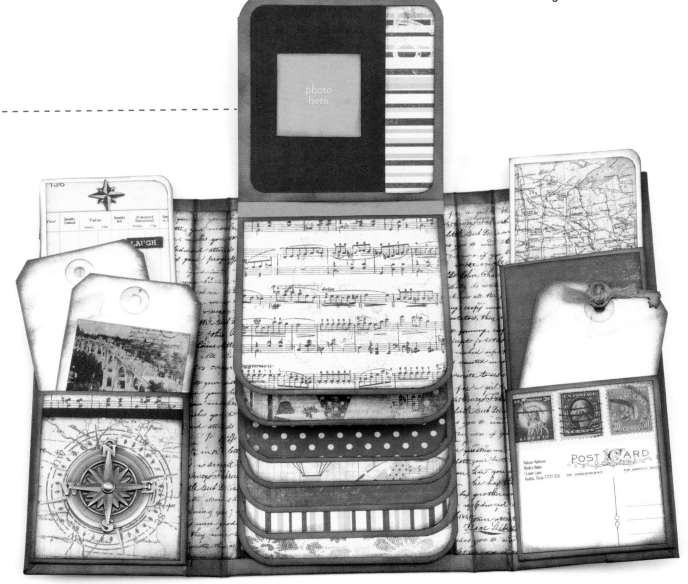

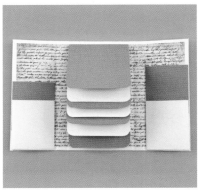

[ Photo 9 ]

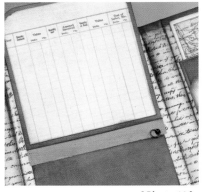

[ Photo 10 ]

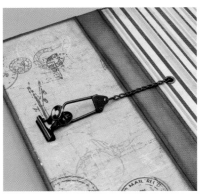

[ Photo 11 ]

**15.** Center and adhere one G pocket to left side of album, 3¼ inches down from top. Decorate front side of pocket with patterned paper as desired. Layer second G pocket on top of first pocket, ⅛ inch up from bottom edge.

Decorate with patterned paper as desired. Repeat for right-hand side of album, adhering one pocket G 1¾ inches down from top and layering second pocket ⅛ inch up from bottom of album (Photo 9).

**16.** Decorate outside of album with patterned paper and embellishments as desired.

**17.** To attach closure, open album and fold up hinged flap pieces. Use an awl or other hole-punching tool to punch a hole 4¼ inches up from bottom and 4½ inches from the right-side edge of the album. Place an eyelet through the hole from the back side of the album and attach following manufacturer's directions using eyelet-setting tool as needed. Remove jump ring from end of swivel clasp chain; thread chain through hole and re-attach jump ring. Open swivel clasp and thread on hinge clip embellishment. Close clasp (Photos 10 and 11). ◀

*Sources: Fair Skies patterned paper set from Farmhouse Paper Company; hinge clip and swivel clasp from Tim Holtz; scoring board and bone folder from Martha Stewart Crafts; paper trimmer from Fiskars; craft knife from Prima Marketing; quick-drying adhesive from 3M; Scor-Tape™ double-sided adhesive from Scor-Pal Products.*

# Bonus Add-Ons

- *You can further embellish your album with tags and folders that slide into the pockets. Make as many as desired to hold photos, journaling and memorabilia.*
- ***Large Tag:** Cut 2½ x 4½-inch piece cardstock. Taper two top corners to create tag shape. Punch ¼-inch hole in center. Embellish as desired.*
- ***Folder:** Cut 5½ x 6¾-inch piece cardstock. Place short edge against top of scoring board. Score at 2¾-inch mark. Round four corners if desired. Embellish inside and outside. Fold and insert into album pocket.*

# All Wrapped Up

You will be amazed at all the space in this mini album. Hidden hinges allow the pockets to flip down, doubling your space for photos and memorabilia.

## Materials

› 7 dark brown sheets of 12 x 12-inch cardstock
› Patterned paper in desired colors
› Chipboard (optional): 1½-inch decorated circle with center hole, 1½ x 2½-inch piece
› Sticky notes
› Alphabet stickers in desired colors
› Embellishments in desired colors
› 2 (¼-inch) eyelets in desired color (optional)
› 32 inches (1mm) black cord (optional)
› Paper piercer (optional)
› Punches (optional): ¼-inch hole, ¾-inch circle, 1½-inch circle, 1¼-inch circle, corner rounder
› Eyelet-setting tool (optional)
› Ruler
› Paper trimmer
› Scoring board
› Bone folder
› Dimensional adhesive
› Quick-drying liquid adhesive
› Double-sided adhesive

*Project note:* Refer to General Instructions for specific techniques as needed. Contrasting cardstock has been used in photos to aid in visual instructions. Use sticky notes to label all cut pieces with the corresponding letter to help identify pieces for scoring and assembly. Decorate finished album using quick-drying and dimensional adhesive as need when adhering embellishments.

## Pieces to Cut
**Cardstock**

Two 6 x 5⅞ inches (A)

Two 7 x 6 inches (B)

Four 5 x 5⅞ inches (C)

Four 7 x 5 inches (D)

Two 1¾ x 6 inches (E)

Two 1¾ x 6 inches (F)

One 1¼ x 6 inches (G)

Two 1¼ x 5 inches (H)

Four 7 x 3½ inches (I)

Six 5 x 4½ inches (J)

Two 5 x 6 inches (K)

## Scoring Instructions

**1.** Place long edge of B against top of scoring board. Score at ½-inch and 6½-inch marks. Repeat for second piece.

**2.** Place long edge of D against the top of scoring board. Score at ½-inch and 6½-inch marks. Repeat for remaining three pieces.

**3.** Place short edge of E against top of scoring board. Score at ½-inch and 1¼-inch marks. Repeat for second piece.

**4.** Place short edge of F against top of scoring board. Score at ½-inch, ⅞-inch and 1¼-inch marks. Repeat for second piece.

**5.** Place short edge of G against top of scoring board. Score at ½-inch and ¾-inch marks.

**6.** Place short edge of H against top of scoring board. Score at ½-inch and ¾-inch marks. Repeat for remaining piece.

**7.** Place long edge of I against top of scoring board. Score at ½-inch and 6½-inch marks. Repeat for remaining three pieces. Place short edge of I against top of scoring board. Score at ½-inch mark. Repeat for remaining three pieces. *Note: The scored lines will cross.*

**8.** Place long edge of J against top of scoring board. Score at ½-inch mark. Repeat for remaining five pieces. Place short edge of J against top of scoring board. Score at ½-inch mark. Repeat for remaining five pieces.

**9.** Place short edge of K against top of scoring board. Score at 1-inch mark. Repeat for remaining piece.

## Top Section Assembly

**1.** Fold both edges of one piece B at score lines. Place double-sided adhesive on edges in the Folded Position (page 4); do not apply adhesive on scored line.

**2.** Adhere piece B from step 1 to piece A, matching 6-inch edges (Fig. 1). ***Note:*** *Piece A is slightly smaller to reduce bulk along the scored and folded edge.* This creates one center page with a pocket on top and bottom. Repeat steps 1 and 2 with remaining pieces A and B for a total of two Center Pages. Mark each as Center Pages; set aside.

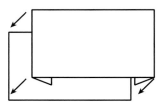

**Fig. 1**

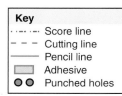

| Key | |
|---|---|
| ·—·—·— | Score line |
| — — — | Cutting line |
| —— | Pencil line |
| ▢ | Adhesive |
| ◉◉ | Punched holes |

**3.** Fold both edges of one piece D at score lines. In the same manner as step 1, place double-sided adhesive on edges in the folded position avoiding scored lines.

**4.** Adhere D to C matching 5-inch edges. Repeat steps 3 and 4 with remaining C and D pieces to create a total of four Side Pages. Mark each as Side Pages; set aside (Fig. 2).

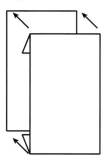
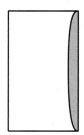

**Fig. 2**

**5.** Taper the four edges of both pieces E. Fold on score lines. Flatten to original size (Fig. 3).

> *Tip*
>
> *After adhering two pieces together, burnish the area with your bone folder to strengthen the bond of the adhesive.*

**Fig. 3**

**6.** Place double-sided adhesive along the right-hand long edge of E. Do not place adhesive on score line. Adhere E under the left-side edge of one Center Page, so the opening pockets of the Center Page are facing up and down. Make sure score line on E is not underneath the Center Page. With same Center Page, repeat with second piece E placing double-sided adhesive on left-hand long edge and adhering under the right-hand edge Center Page. Decorate Center Page with patterned paper as desired (Photo 1).

**7.** Place double-sided adhesive tape along the left edge of E on both the front and back sides; avoid placing adhesive on scored lines. Open a pocket on one Side Page and slide over E, lining up edge of side pocket with score line. ***Note:*** *Do not slide hinge in so far that score line is covered.* Repeat on other side of Center Page using second Side Page to create a Top Section. Decorate Side Pages with patterned paper as desired (Photo 2).

**8.** On one piece I, cut out the two squares created by the overlapping score marks. Fold along three score lines (Fig. 4a). Place double-sided adhesive along edge of three score lines in Folded Position (Fig. 4b).

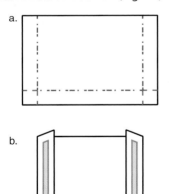

**Fig. 4**

**9.** Adhere piece I from step 8 to left-hand edge of Center Page creating a pocket that opens toward the right-hand side of the album (Photo 3). Decorate pocket with patterned paper as desired.

**10.** On two pieces J, cut out the squares created by the overlapping score marks. Lay the pockets on your work surface so you have a left and right pocket (Fig. 5).

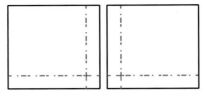

**Fig. 5**

**11.** On the right-hand piece J from step 10, make a mark 2 inches up from the bottom score line on the right-hand edge and 2 inches in from the left score line on the top edge. Draw a diagonal line between the marks and cut, creating a diagonal pocket. Repeat on left-hand piece J using left edge bottom and right edge top to create a mirrored pocket. Fold flaps under along scored edges (Fig. 6).

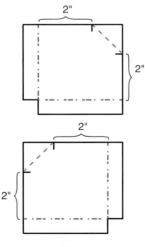

**Fig. 6**

**12.** Place double-sided adhesive along scored edges of both pockets while in the Folded Position. Adhere pockets to Side Pages as shown. Decorate pockets with patterned paper as desired (Photo 4).

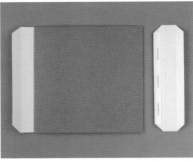

[ Photo 1 ]

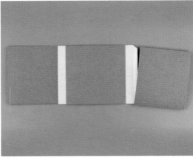

[ Photo 2 ]

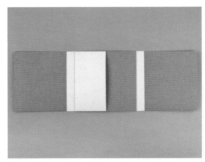

[ Photo 3 ]

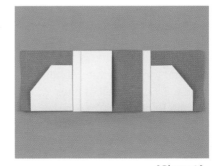

[ Photo 4 ]

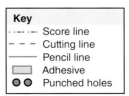

| Key | |
|---|---|
| ·–··–· | Score line |
| – – – | Cutting line |
| —— | Pencil line |
| ▭ | Adhesive |
| ⬤⬤ | Punched holes |

**13.** Taper the top and bottom edges of K from the score line to the 1-inch edge. Fold along score lines. Flatten to original size (Fig. 7).

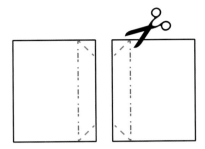

**Fig. 7**

**14.** Apply double-sided adhesive along 1-inch flap in the Extended Position (page 4). Slide a taped flap into outer opening of a Side Pocket up to score line. Do not slide in so far that score line is covered. Repeat for other side. Decorate flaps with patterned paper as desired (Photo 5).

## Bottom Section Assembly

**1.** Taper the four edges of F. Accordion-fold on the three score lines. Repeat for second piece F (Fig. 8).

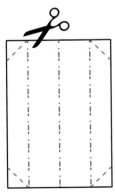

**Fig. 8**

**2.** Lay piece F with center valley of accordion fold facing up (Photo 6).

**3.** Follow steps 6 and 7 of Top Section Assembly using set-aside Center Page, two Side Pages and two accordion-folded F pieces instead of E pieces. Make sure the valley of the accordion-folded pieces is facing up.

**4.** Repeat step 8 of Top Section Assembly and adhere as shown creating a pocket that opens to the top of the album. Decorate Pocket with patterned paper as desired (Photo 7).

**5.** Repeat steps 10 and 11 of Top Section Assembly to create diagonal pockets. Reverse pockets and adhere as shown. Decorate flaps with patterned paper as desired (Photo 8).

## Assemble Top to Bottom Section

**1.** Taper all edges of G and H as shown in Fig. 9. Fold along the score lines. Flatten to original size.

**Fig. 9**

**2.** Lay the Top Section Assembly on the worktable. Lay an H hinge under each Side Pocket and a G hinge under the Center Pocket. Lay the Bottom Section below the hinges (Photo 9).

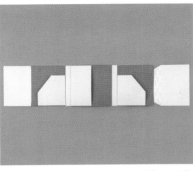

[ Photo 5 ]

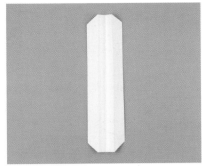

[ Photo 6 ]

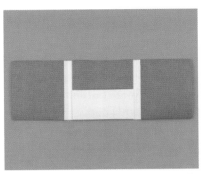

[ Photo 7 ]

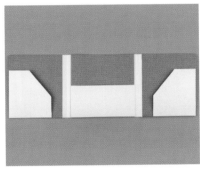

[ Photo 8 ]

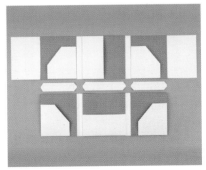

[ Photo 9 ]

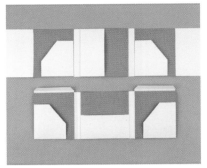

[ Photo 10 ]

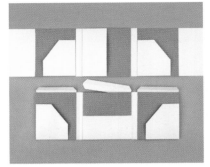

[ Photo 11a ]

[ Photo 11b ]

**3.** Apply double-sided adhesive to the bottom edge of H. Adhere to the back of the left-hand Side Pocket of the Bottom Section, lining up edge of pocket with score line. Make sure score line is not hidden beneath pocket. Repeat for the second H, adhering to the back of the right-hand Side Pocket (Photo 10).

**4.** Apply double-sided adhesive to the bottom edge of G on both the front and back sides. Slide taped edge into pocket of the Bottom Assembly Center Page to adhere (Photo 11a and 11b).

**5.** Assemble Top Section to G and H in same manner (Photo 12).

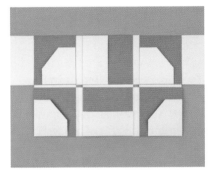

[ Photo 12 ]

**6.** Fold in Flaps on left and right sides of Top Assembly. Flip bottom section closed over top section. Decorate these center and side pages with patterned paper as desired (Photo 13).

**7.** Repeat step 8 of Top Section. Adhere to Center page creating pocket that opens toward top of album (Photo 14).

**8.** Repeat steps 10 and 11 from Top Section Assembly to create diagonal pockets, this time adhering so pocket diagonals face each other. Decorate pockets with patterned paper as desired (Photo 15).

**9.** Fold right-hand side of album to center. Repeat steps 8 and 9 of Top Section Assembly, adhering the pocket to the back side of the folded right-hand Side Page so it opens to the right-hand side (Photo 16).

**10.** Decorate with patterned paper as desired. Add dimensional embellishment to all pages as desired.

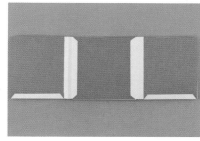

[ Photo 13 ]

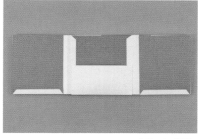

[ Photo 14 ]

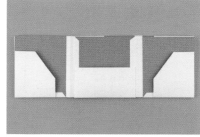

[ Photo 15 ]

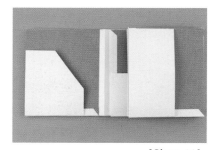

[ Photo 16 ]

**11.** To fold album, fold Bottom Section up to cover Top Section. Fold right-hand side to center. Fold left-hand side to center.

### Cord Closure (optional)

**1.** Use double-sided adhesive to adhere 1½ x 2½-inch piece of patterned paper to a 1½ x 2½-inch piece of chipboard creating a back closure piece.

**2.** Punch two ¼-inch holes through center of back closure piece as shown. Set eyelets in holes following manufacturer's instructions (Fig. 10).

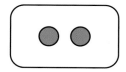

**Fig. 10**

**3.** Loop cord down through one hole and up through second hole. Thread tails through loop. Tighten (Fig. 11).

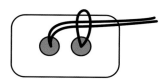

**Fig. 11**

**4.** Using a strong adhesive, adhere back closure to back of album; let dry (Fig. 12).

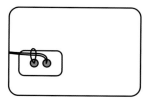

**Fig. 12**

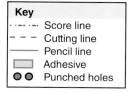

Key
- ·–··–· Score line
- – – Cutting line
- —— Pencil line
- ▢ Adhesive
- ⬤⬤ Punched holes

# Bonus Add-Ons

- *You can further embellish your album and give it even more spaces for photos, text or memorabilia by making sliding tags that fit into the various-size pockets. Make as many sliding tags as fit comfortably into your album. Remember, when you begin to add photos, you album will bulk up quickly.*
- ***Large Tag:*** *Cut 5¾ x 5½-inch piece cardstock. Round four corners. Embellish as desired. Slide into large pockets in album.*
- ***Medium Tag:*** *Cut 3⅛ x 5¼-inch piece cardstock. Clip top two corners to form tag shape. Punch ¼-inch hole in center top. Embellish as desired.*
- ***Small Tag:*** *Cut 3 x 4-inch piece cardstock. Round all four corners. Embellish or add photos.*

**5.** Punch a 1½-inch circle from desired patterned paper and a ¾-inch circle from dark brown cardstock. Using 1½-inch circle and 1¼-inch circle punch, create a circle frame from dark brown cardstock. Referring to completed project photo, layer and adhere punched circles, frame and 1½-inch chipboard circle together.

**6.** Using hole in chipboard circle as a guide, pierce a hole through center of layered circle piece and insert brad. Punch a ¾-inch circle from chipboard. Adhere to back of layered circle piece. Adhere to album cover using strong adhesive. Let dry. ◀

***Sources:*** *Snap patterned paper and paper/chipboard embellishments from Simple Stories; ruler and twine from Tim Holtz; scoring board and bone folder from Martha Stewart Crafts; paper trimmer from Fiskars; Glossy Accents dimensional adhesive from Ranger Industries Inc.; quick-drying adhesive from 3M; Scor-Tape™ double-sided adhesive from Scor-Pal Products.*

# Side By Side

This off-set, gatefold album is the perfect place to keep your most treasured photos and memorabilia. Display it on an end table as a conversation piece or give as a gift.

*Project note: Refer to General Instructions for specific techniques as needed. Contrasting cardstock has been used in photos to aid in visual instructions. Use sticky notes to label all cut pieces with the corresponding letter to help identify pieces for scoring and assembly.*

## Pieces to Cut

### Chipboard

One 8½ x 6 inches (A)

One 6½ x 6 inches (B)

One 4½ x 6 inches (C)

Two ½ x 6 inches (D)

### Solid Cardstock

Two 2½ x 6 inches (E)

Two 5¾ x 3 inches (F)

One 7 x 5¾ inches (G)

One 6¾ x 6 inches (H)

One 5½ x 9¾ inches (I)

One 4½ x 3½ inches (J)

One 3 x 6¾ inches (K)

One 9½ x 5½ inches (L)

Four 5 x 6 inches (M)

Four 3½ x 7 inches (N)

One 7½ x 5½ inches (O)

One 5½ x 5½ inches (P)

One 12 x 1½ inches (Q)

### Patterned Cardstock

One 12 x 7½ inches (R)

One 7 x 7½ inches (S)

One 5 x 7½ inches (T)

One 8½ x 5¾ inches (U)

One 6⅜ x 5¾ inches (V)

One 4⅜ x 5¾ inches (W)

## Materials

› 12 x 12-inch chipboard
› 6 (12 x 12-inch) solid cardstock
› 3 (12 x 12-inch) patterned cardstock, plus pieces to decorate as desired
› Sticky notes
› ¼-inch eyelets
› 3 large jump rings
› 16 inches ¼-inch-wide elastic
› Punches: ¼-inch hole (or awl), corner rounder
› Eyelet-setting tool (optional)
› Ruler
› Paper trimmer
› Scissors
› Scoring board
› Bone folder
› Craft knife
› Quick-drying liquid adhesive
› ¼-inch-wide double-sided adhesive

## Scoring Instructions

**1.** Place short edge of F against top of scoring board. Score at 1-inch, 1½-inch and 2-inch marks. Repeat for remaining piece.

**2.** Place long edge of H against top of scoring board. Score at ½-inch and 6¼-inch marks.

**3.** Place long edge of I against top of scoring board. Score at 5¾-inch mark. Place the short edge against top of scoring board. Score at ½-inch and 5-inch marks.

**4.** Place short edge of J against top of scoring board. Score at 1-inch mark.

**5.** Place long edge of K against top of scoring board. Score at ½-inch and 6¼-inch marks.

**6.** Place long edge of L against top of scoring board. Score at ½-inch and 9-inch marks. Place short edge against top of scoring board and score at ½-inch mark.

**7.** Place short edge of M against top of scoring board. Score at ¾-inch and 1-inch marks. Repeat for remaining three pieces.

**8.** Place long edge of N against top of scoring board and score at ½-inch and 6½-inch marks. Place short edge against top of scoring board. Score at ½-inch mark. Repeat for remaining three pieces.

**9.** Place long edge of O against top of scoring board. Score at ½-inch and 7-inch marks. Place short edge against top of scoring board and score at ½-inch mark.

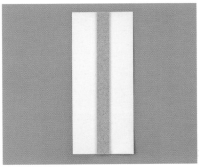

[ Photo 1 ]

[ Photo 2 ]

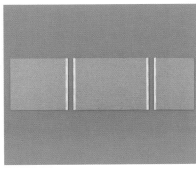

[ Photo 3 ]

**10.** Place one edge of P against top of scoring board. Score at ½-inch and 5-inch marks. Rotate 90 degrees and score at ½-inch mark.

### Assembly Instructions

**1.** On one piece E, measure and mark a line 1 inch from the left edge. Repeat for second piece E (Fig. 1).

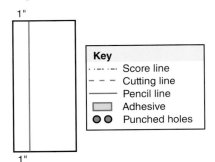

1"

1"

**Key**
- · – · · – · Score line
- – – – Cutting line
- ——— Pencil line
- ▢ Adhesive
- ⬤ ⬤ Punched holes

**Fig. 1**

**2.** Adhere one piece D to E aligning edge of chipboard to right-hand side of pencil line. This will center the chipboard piece on the cardstock. Repeat with second E piece (Photo 1).

**3.** On one piece E, apply a strip of ¼-inch tape along both sides of the chipboard. Keep tape snug against chipboard. Apply a second piece ¼-inch tape along both outside edges of the cardstock. Repeat for second piece E (Photo 2).

**4.** Put tape along both 6-inch edges of A. Put tape along the right-hand 6-inch edge of B and the left-hand 6-inch edge of C (Photo 3).

**5.** Remove paper backing from tape on one edge of A. Remove paper backing from tape on one outside edge of E. Flip A upside down so tape is facing down. Adhere A to E, lining up chipboard with edge of tape on E that is nearest the center ½-inch chipboard. Pieces will overlap about ½-inch. **Note:** *After adhering two pieces together, burnish the area with your bone folder to strengthen the bond of the adhesive.* Repeat for other edge A (Photo 4).

**6.** Attach B to left-hand side of album and C to right-hand side of album in same manner as in step 5. Pieces will overlap about ½ inch (Photo 5).

**7.** Flip album upside down. Apply tape around perimeter of entire cover. Apply good tape coverage to all interior areas of rectangle (Photo 6).

**8.** On the patterned side (or side determined to be the front if double-sided) of piece R, measure and draw a pencil line ½ inch along both 7½-inch sides.

[ Photo 4 ]

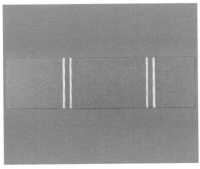

[ Photo 5 ]

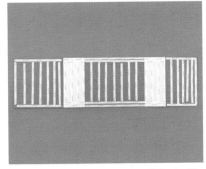

[ Photo 6 ]

**9.** Adhere S to R along the right 7½-inch edge, overlapping S onto R and matching pencil line. Adhere T to R along the left 7½-inch edge, overlapping T onto R and matching pencil line. Your finished rectangle should measure 23 x 7½ inches. This is the cover for the album. If using cardstock that is two-sided, determine which side will be the cover. Mark the other side as Back (Fig. 2).

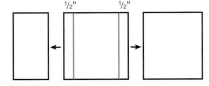

**Fig. 2**

**10.** On the back side of the 23 x 7½-inch piece from step 9, draw lines ¾ inch in from each edge (Fig. 3).

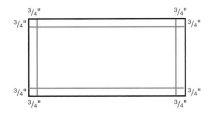

**Fig. 3**

**11.** Remove paper backing from tape on chipboard piece from

step 7. Align piece B with piece S along pencil lines and press down to secure chipboard to cardstock (Photo 7). **Note:** *If chipboard extends over pencil lines slightly, that's OK; there is enough margin to wrap around the edges. If the chipboard piece does not extend to reach the end pencil line, simply trim excess cardstock leaving a ¾-inch margin.*

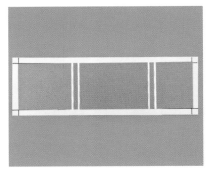

[ Photo 7 ]

**12.** Apply tape around the ¾-inch perimeter of the cardstock. Measure 1¼ inches from each corner and make a pencil mark. Draw a line between marks. You should have about ⅛ inch between the line and the corner of your chipboard. Adjust line if necessary before cutting miter. Repeat for all four corners and cut along lines (Photo 8).

[ Photo 8 ]

**13.** Remove paper backing from tape around perimeter and from between small chipboard pieces. Wrap one long edge of paper around chipboard. Keep edges tight and press to secure. Press the excess cardstock at the miter down with a bone folder or your fingernail to secure around the corner of the chipboard. Fold the next side. Work your way around the cover, completing each corner in the same manner (Photo 9).

[ Photo 9 ]

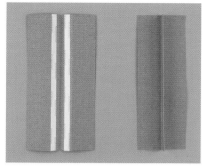

[ Photo 10 ]

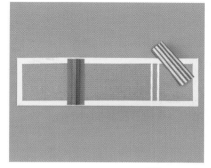

[ Photo 11 ]

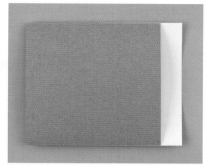

[ Photo 12 ]

**14.** On one piece F, place tape on the two ½-inch spaces created by the score lines. Remove paper backing from tape and fold together on the center score line. Fold the 1-inch pieces away from each other forming the hinge. Repeat for second piece (Photo 10).

**15.** Place tape on the 1-inch spaces on the back side of hinge F. Center and adhere hinge to ½-inch chipboard spine on album. Repeat with second hinge on other side of album. Gently burnish hinges down into sticky spaces on each side of chipboard hinge. This will identify the folding edges of the spine on your album (Photo 11).

**16.** Fold H on score lines. Place tape on two flaps in the Folded Position (page 4).

**17.** Decorate G with patterned paper as desired. Adhere H to left edge of G so that the pocket opening faces left and right (Photo 12).

*Tip*

• *Create glitter strips by applying double-sided adhesive to black cardstock. Remove backing; sprinkle with glitter. Cut strip out; adhere to scrapbook cover.*

**18.** Taper each end of tab of left-hand hinge about ¼ inch (Fig. 4).

Fig. 4

| Key | |
|---|---|
| –·–·– | Score line |
| – – – | Cutting line |
| —— | Pencil line |
| ▭ | Adhesive |
| ●● | Punched holes |

**19.** Put tape on both outer edges of hinge tab. Remove backing paper from tape. Slide the pocket created in step 17 over hinge, leaving about ⅛ inch between pocket edge and base of hinge. *Note: The ⅛ inch allows the pocket to fold without binding.* Place a line of quick-drying liquid adhesive along the pocket left edge near the hinge to seal the pocket shut (Photos 13 and 14).

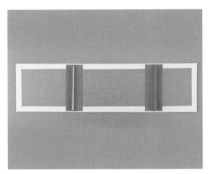

[ Photo 13 ]

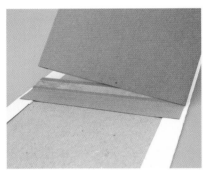

[ Photo 14 ]

**20.** Lay I on worktable with long section at top. Cut along the long vertical score lines to the horizontal score line. Finish the cut by tapering to the outside edge. Repeat for opposite side (Fig. 5).

**21.** Fold flaps of bottom section in along score lines. Apply tape to flaps in the Folded Position. Fold and adhere bottom section to top section creating envelope pocket (Fig. 6).

**22.** Fold J on score line. Flatten to original size. Taper edges slightly. Apply tape to the 1-inch section. (Fig. 7).

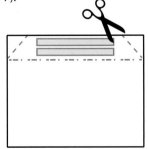

**Fig. 7**

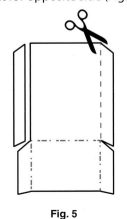

**Fig. 5**

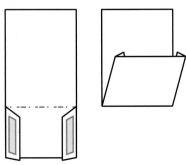

**Fig. 6**

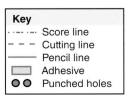

| Key | |
| --- | --- |
| –·–·– | Score line |
| – – – | Cutting line |
| ——— | Pencil line |
| ▭ | Adhesive |
| ●● | Punched holes |

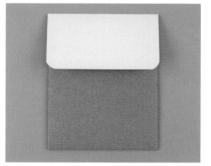

[ Photo 15 ]

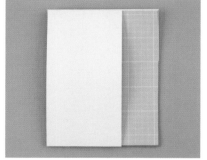

[ Photo 16 ]

[ Photo 17 ]

**23.** Adhere J to back of pocket matching score line and top edge of pocket. Use corner rounder or scissors to round edges of pocket flap if desired. Decorate both sides of envelope and envelope flap with patterned paper if desired (Photo 15).

**24.** Fold K on score lines. Apply tape to the flaps in the folded position. Adhere to left-hand side on front (opposite side of flap closure) of envelope pocket (Photo 16).

**25.** Taper each end of tab on right-hand hinge about ¼ inch referring to Fig. 5. Put tape on both sides of the right-hand hinge tab. With envelope opening facing to the right-hand side, slide pocket created in step 24 over hinge tab, leaving ⅛ inch between pocket edge and hinge base. Press to secure. Place a line of quick-drying liquid adhesive along the left edge of K near the hinge to seal the pocket shut (Photo 17).

**26.** Fold hinge flaps left and right to expose center section of album. Center and adhere U over chipboard.

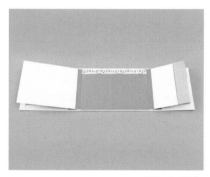

[ Photo 18 ]

**27.** On L, cut out squares created by crossing score lines. Fold on score lines. Apply tape to flaps in the folded position. Adhere pocket to bottom of center section (Photo 18).

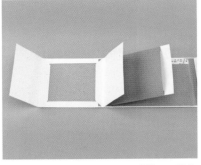

[ Photo 19 ]

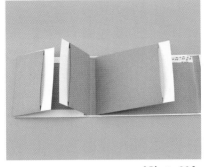

[ Photo 20 ]

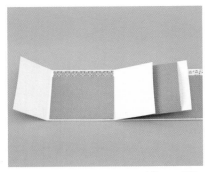

[ Photo 21 ]

**28.** On one piece M, taper two corners from outer score line to edge of cardstock. Repeat for remaining three pieces (Fig. 8).

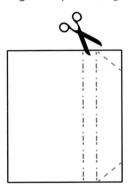

**Fig. 8**

| Key | |
|---|---|
| ·─·─·─ | Score line |
| ─ ─ ─ | Cutting line |
| ──── | Pencil line |
| ▭ | Adhesive |
| ◉ ◉ | Punched holes |

**29.** Fold two pieces M on both score lines. Place tape on ¾-inch space created by score line. To adhere one flap, line up the score line closest to the tapered edge with the left-hand edge of the album. Repeat on opposite edge of left-hand section, making sure to keep flap about ¼ inch away from previously completed hinge. Decorate flaps with patterned paper as desired (Photo 19).

**30.** On two pieces N, cut out square created by intersecting score lines. Fold on score lines. Place tape on flaps in folded position. Fold flaps from step 29 toward each other. Adhere one pocket on the left-hand flap with the opening facing to the right. Adhere second pocket on the right-hand flap with the opening facing to the left (Photo 20).

**31.** Center and adhere V to chipboard center on left-hand section of album.

**32.** On piece O, cut out squares created by intersecting score lines. Fold along score lines. Place tape on flaps in folded position. Adhere pocket to bottom of V (Photo 21).

**33.** Repeat steps 29 and 30 to adhere flaps and pockets to the right-hand section of album.

[ Photo 22 ]

**34.** Center and adhere W to chipboard center on right-hand side of album. Repeat step 32 using piece P to create pocket and adhering to W.

**35.** To create bellyband closure, cut elastic into two 8-inch pieces. On piece Q punch four ¼-inch holes for eyelets ⅜ inch from edges of band (Fig. 9).

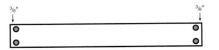

**Fig. 9**

**36.** From the front side of the band, thread elastic through hole ¼ inch and then insert eyelet through hole. Secure eyelet following manufacturer's directions. The eyelet will hold the elastic. Repeat for remaining elastic ends and eyelets (Photo 22).

**37.** Decorate album with patterned paper and embellishments as desired. ❮

***Sources:*** *Love Letters patterned papers and Lover Letters Buttons (charms) from Bo-Bunny Press; scoring board and bone folder from Martha Stewart Crafts; paper trimmer from Fiskars; craft knife from Prima Marketing; quick-drying adhesive from 3M; Scor-Tape™ double-sided adhesive from Scor-Pal Products.*

# Bonus Add-Ons

- *You can further embellish your album with tags that slide into the pockets. Make as many as desired to hold photos, journaling and memorabilia.*
- ***Large Tag:*** *Cut 6¼ x 5¼-inch piece cardstock. Round corners. Embellish as desired.*
- ***Medium Tag:*** *Cut 4 x 5½-inch piece cardstock. Round corners. Embellish as desired.*
- ***Small Tag:*** *Cut 3 x 5½-inch piece cardstock. Round corners. Embellish as desired.*
- ***Large Folder:*** *Cut 8½ x 5½-inch piece cardstock. Place the long edge against the top of your scoring board and score at 4¼-inch mark. Round four corners. Fold along score line. Embellish as desired.*
- ***Small Folder:*** *Cut 6 x 3½-inch piece cardstock. Place the long edge against the top of your scoring board and score at 3-inch mark. Fold along score line. Embellish as desired.*

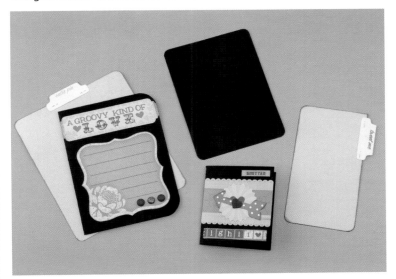

# Buyer's Guide

**3M**
(800) 328-6276
www.scotchbrand.com

**Bo-Bunny Press**
(801) 771-4010
www.bobunny.com

**Farmhouse Paper Company**
(918) 506-4416
http://farmhousepaper.
myshopify.com

**Fiskars**
(918) 506-4416
www2.fiskars.com

**Martha Stewart Crafts**
www.eksuccessbrands.com/
marthastewartcrafts

**Prima Marketing Inc.**
(909) 627-5532
www.primamarketinginc.com

**Ranger Industries Inc.**
(732) 389-3535
www.rangerink.com

**Scor-Pal Products**
(877) 629-9908
www.scor-pal.com

**Simple Stories**
(801) 737-3242
http://simplestories.typepad.
com/simple_stories

**Tim Holtz**
www.timholtz.com

*The Buyer's Guide listings are
provided as a service to our readers
and should not be considered an
endorsement from this publication.*

Annie's®  *Interactive Mini Scrapbooks* is published by Annie's, 306 East Parr Road, Berne, IN 46711. Printed in USA. Copyright © 2013 Annie's.
All rights reserved. This publication may not be reproduced in part or in whole without written permission from the publisher.

**RETAIL STORES:** If you would like to carry this pattern book or any other Annie's publication, visit AnniesWSL.com.

Every effort has been made to ensure that the instructions in this pattern book are complete and accurate. We cannot, however, take responsibility for
human error, typographical mistakes or variations in individual work. Please visit AnniesCustomerCare.com to check for pattern updates.

ISBN: 978-1-59635-817-1

1 2 3 4 5 6 7 8 9